A descendant of the prophet Mohammed, Hussein has survived a dozen attempts on his life. His politically turbulent reign has been punctuated by several troubled marriages. In recent years, though, he has found happiness with his fourth wife, Queen Noor. She is a former American college girl, Lisa Halaby, who has given Hussein four more children and has gained the respect of the Jordanians.

FORGING A WARRIOR KING

GROOMED TO BE KING BY HIS GRANDFATHER, HUSSEIN SAW THE OLD MAN SHOT DEAD AT HIS SIDE. HIS FATHER WAS THEN DECLARED INCAPABLE OF RULING AND HUSSEIN, STILL IN HIS TEENS, SUCCEEDED TO THE THRONE

👑 *Hussein made his first public appearance above in the arms of a nurse just a few weeks after his birth in his father's relatively modest house in Amman. Nearby, in the Raghadan Palace, lived his grandfather, Abdullah, Emir of Transjordan below. His family, the Hashemites, trace their descent directly through 13 centuries to Fatima, daughter of the Prophet Mohammed*

T HE HASHEMITE KINGDOM OF JORDAN WAS founded in 1920. Known then as Transjordan, its first ruler was Abdullah, Hussein's grandfather. Transjordan, like all modern Arab states, was born of an agreement between Britain and France which split the Arab countries into different 'areas of influence'. This took place after the Arabs had overthrown the rule of the Ottoman Turks.

Abdullah was not a Jordanian; he was a Hashemite, descended from the traditional guardians of Mecca and Medina. But he was an Arab, and, after years of Turkish domination, the Arab people of Transjordan accepted him as their ruler.

The Arab tribes who had fought brilliantly under Sharif Hussein, assisted by T.E. Lawrence ('Lawrence of Arabia'), were bitter at what they saw as a double-cross by Britain and France. However, Abdullah, who had led one of the Arab armies during the final campaign, when his brother, Feisal, and Lawrence had marched into Damascus in 1918, was content to rule Jordan under British patronage.

Three years before the foundation of Transjordan, the British Government, in the Balfour Declaration, sanctioned the creation of a national Jewish homeland in neighbouring Palestine. It was an act that was to bring about Abdullah's death by an assassin's bullet; and it was to have a profound influence on the life of King Hussein.

Abdullah ruled an arid land of desert and scrub, stretching from the Gulf of Aqaba in the south to the Syrian borders in the north. For much of his reign, the country was inhabited mainly by Bedouin people, many of whom settled in the capital, the small and dusty city of Amman. Nomadic Bedouins also moved freely over the deserts in the north and south.

A King is born

It was in Amman that Hussein was born to Abdullah's elder son, Talal, on 14 November 1935. He was the eldest of four children, with two brothers, Mohammed and Hassan, and a sister, Basma.

Abdullah was a fierce, hawkish warrior who ruled by an instinctive combination of force, guile and support from the many Bedouin leaders whose tribes made up the vast majority of the Jordanian population. By contrast, Talal was a thoughtful, well-read man,

Camera Press

👑 *Young Hussein* left *was a quiet, happy child, who grew up in an atmosphere of warmth and security. As the first-born, he seemed to be the special favourite of his mother, Zein*

👑 *Hussein's father, Talal, the heir to the throne, was keen to pass on to his eldest son his own passion for Arab history, culture and traditions. Talal was an accomplished horseman, like his Bedouin ancestors, and taught the young Hussein to ride at an early age* below

'quiet, contemplative little boy', who did not shine academically although he excelled at English and Arabic poetry. One of his friends at school was a mischievous boy, Zeid Rifai, who was later to become Prime Minister of Jordan.

Hussein's early life was happy and secure. There was no indication that the little boy who walked unguarded, carrying his satchel to the school 200 yards from his house, would one day be the target of several assassination attempts, or that tragedy was already beginning to stalk his life.

Concerned at what he saw as Talal's weakness, Abdullah made no secret of the fact that he saw Hussein, not his own son, as the country's future leader. Conflicting plans for Hussein's education led to a great clash of wills between grandfather and father.

Jordan depended almost entirely on Great Britain for its income and Abdullah wanted his grandson to have an English public school education and to be a soldier. Talal, who had suffered humiliation at Harrow – where he had been thrown into the swimming pool in his first

deeply imbued with Arab history. The contrast was such that occasional conflict was inevitable between the two men. Abdullah had some doubts about his son's suitability as a future ruler of the kingdom.

Mother's love

Hussein's mother, Zein, is a woman of strong personality, although, in the true Arab tradition, she apparently demurred to both Abdullah and her husband. Later, after Abdullah's death, she was to become very much a power behind Hussein's throne. However, her main concern during his infancy and childhood was to ensure the maximum happiness for her eldest son. It was almost as if she knew that the child would, at an early age, be thrown into the maelstrom of kingship in one of the most troubled parts of the world.

Zein was attentive to the demands of all her children, but Royal observers in Jordan noted that Hussein was the most cosseted, with Zein keeping him safely away from the frequent and heated arguments between grandfather and father.

Talal and his family lived in a house of grey stone on a hillside overlooking the city. Although it was bigger than most of Amman's middle-class dwellings and had a stable block (Talal was a keen horseman), it was suburban in aspect and so was family life.

Schooling

After some years in a nursery school, Hussein attended the Christian Missionary school close to his home. His teachers described him as a

Popperfoto

👑 *Hussein's mother, Zein far left was Talal's cousin. Although she had grown to young womanhood in the sophisticated surroundings of Cairo, she quickly accustomed herself, after her marriage in 1934, to the more traditional constraints of the Transjordanian court, always deferring to her husband and father-in-law. Talal left, a gentle and contemplative man, often quarrelled with his father, the Emir, who was said to prefer Talal's extrovert half-brother, Naif*

week – sought the intellectual life for his son.

Hussein was deeply attached to his father. He rode with him into the desert and accompanied him on duck shooting expeditions. Unlike Abdullah, Talal took a 'level view' of Britain's role in his country's history, and sought to stress to Hussein that he was an Arab first and foremost. Talal spent many hours reading and discusssing Arabic history and culture with his three sons.

It was through his father, however, that

👑 *Transjordan became fully independent in 1946, and on 25 May Emir Abdullah became King. The crowds who flocked to Amman for his inauguration included many Jordanian women who flouted tradition by appearing in public without a veil below*

Kirkbride never fully trusted Talal to keep Jordan under Britain's influence but he was always a close friend of Talal and his family. As a friend, Kirkbride went duck shooting with Talal and Hussein at an oasis east of Amman and noted how 'Hussein's small figure would be almost lost in a pair of plus fours.'

Tragedy came in the form of a schizophrenic illness that struck Talal in the early 1940s, turning Hussein's gentle father into a man of almost uncontrollable fury. In the early stages,

'Hussein's small figure would be almost lost in a pair of plus fours'

PETER SNOW ON YOUNG HUSSEIN

Hussein came to know Sir Alec Kirkbride, the British resident minister who wielded immense political influence over King Abdullah, and John Glubb. Glubb, who became known as Glubb Pasha, had formed and now commanded the Arab Legion, an army made up mainly of Bedouins who were fiercely loyal to Abdullah and fought off several rebellions. Hussein's boyish respect for John Bagot Glubb was profound. Little did he know that one day he would be forced to dismiss Glubb from his service.

The Illustrated

the family noticed no more than odd 'moods'; but then the condition worsened, and Talal would become a man possessed, throwing fits of anger that frightened his family, especially his eldest son, who was then still a schoolboy in Amman. Abdullah's worries about Talal increased and it became clear that the mantle of ruler would fall upon the young Hussein.

School in Egypt

Abdullah knew that his country's economy was entirely dependent on Britain. He insisted that the boy should attend a British public school. Hussein was sent to Victoria College in Alexandria, Egypt, where he shared a dormitory with 30 other boys and lived a spartan life with cold showers each morning. Hussein took well to public school life; he played football and cricket and won a medal for fencing but he recalls that he was 'endlessly poor'.

Conflict over Israel

It was in 1948 that the whole of the Middle East was thrown into turmoil by the war between the Arab states and the emerging state of Israel. Abdullah had always been reluctant to take part in this war. Indeed, he had taken part in secret negotiations with Israeli leaders, a fact that was to count heavily against him in the Arab community. The Arabs were defeated. Jordan,

Illustrated London News

which had fought more fiercely than most, was flooded with Palestinian refugees.

Abdullah had entrusted a close friend, Abdullah al Tell, with the arrangements for the talks with the Israelis. Tell, piqued at being denied promotion, took the documents to Cairo. Here, long standing political enemies, now backed by Palestinian refugee leaders, were hatching a plot to kill the Jordanian ruler.

⚜ Hussein was not quite 16 when King Abdullah was killed before his eyes in the Al Aqsa mosque in Jerusalem. The assassin was shot dead by the King's bodyguards; his riddled body lay unregarded in the mosque above after Hussein was removed to safety

KING ABDULLAH

Few men have had more influence on Hussein than his grandfather, King Abdullah *right,* with Glubb Pasha. A leading member of the Hashemite family, the traditional guardians of the Holy Cities of Mecca and Medina, Abdullah was the son of Sharif Hussein, King of Hejaz, the area south of Jordan where these cities lie. Abdullah's brother, Feisal, became King of Iraq.

Many people believe that the wild Arab leader portrayed by Anthony Quinn in the film *Lawrence of Arabia* was based on Abdullah. Abdullah certainly had hawklike features and great charisma, but, unlike Quinn's character, he had no part in the liberation of Damascus from Ottoman rule. He spent much of the war nearer home, fighting the Turks at Medina and Taif.

Though perhaps seen by the British as something of a schemer, Abdullah was an astute and pragmatic man. When he became the first ruler of Transjordan, he was acclaimed by the people as their King and leader.

Abdullah was an extrovert with a great sense of humour who lived life to the full and spent more time than most rulers in the company of poets and writers. His son Talal, King Hussein's father, was a much less colourful character

Hulton Picture Company

ASSASSINATION

Despite continual warnings of a plot to murder him at prayer, Abdullah insisted on attending the Aqsa mosque in Jerusalem with his grandson. Hussein, still at college, had just been made an honorary captain, as a reward for his fencing prowess, and was wearing his Arab Legion uniform. As the King entered the building a young man stepped out from behind a door and shot him in the head. It was 20 July 1951.

Hussein tried to grab the assassin, who turned towards him and fired a single shot. The bullet glanced off a medal on Hussein's chest. It was to be his first escape from death. The gunman was shot down by Abdullah's bodyguard. Around his neck was a talisman that read, 'Kill, and thou shalt be safe'. Abdullah's body was flown back to Amman.

Preparing to be king

A separate aircraft was sent to fetch Hussein. The pilot, a Scotsman, Squadron Leader Jock Dalgleish, found Hussein alone and desperate with worry. The boy's father was undergoing treatment in Switzerland; his grandfather was dead. At that moment, he had no-one to turn to. Dalgleish put his arms around young Hussein and said, 'I'll look after you, son.' Thus began a friendship which has lasted to this day. Hussein was not to return to the Egyptian college in the city of Alexandria.

Hussein's uncle Naif, Talal's half-brother, was appointed Regent, but, despite his illness and his anti-British ravings during his bouts of madness, Talal was, briefly, to be King. Both Kirkbride and the Jordanian Prime Minister had recognized that Hussein had the kingly qualities that Abdullah had already noted.

The young Prince was taken on a tour of the country, meeting the Bedouin chiefs, whom he impressed, not merely with gifts, but with his soldierly bearing and authority and his charming good manners. Two months after Abdullah's assassination, Talal became King on 6 September 1951, despite a plot by Naif to assume the throne by a coup. The coup was rapidly put down by Glubb's army. No-one really believed that Talal could reign for very long, and it was essential that Hussein should be well groomed for the role of King.

'A determined fellow, but limited in his academic ability'

HUSSEIN'S HOUSEMASTER AT HARROW

Abdullah had always wanted Hussein to go to Talal's old school. His British advisers arranged for the boy to spend the last year of his public school life at Harrow. Unlike his father, he was relatively happy in the school which produced Winston Churchill, among others. His English was good but he found it hard to communicate with his schoolmates. They had already been at Harrow for three years and had little time for the little Arab Prince, or other newcomers.

Topham

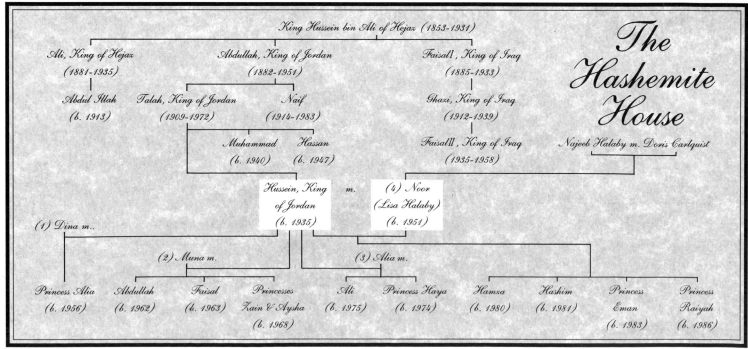

HARROW

It is not surprising that Hussein was sent to Harrow School *right*, in north-west London, which along with Eton ranks as Britain's premier public school. His father, Talal, was sent there and hated it, but he nonetheless saw great value in the spartan regime for his son. Hussein himself had a much happier time at the school, and subsequently sent his own son, Abdullah, to Harrow.

Why this curious paradox? The reason is the intensity and breadth of the education offered by the school, where scholars are still expected to study hard, take cold showers and live relatively spartan lives.

Hussein did not shine academically, but he has agreed privately that his Harrow education was a vital preparation for kingship. Not only was the regime of the school character-building, but Harrow offered future Kings the chance to form influential relationships with those who would go on to play leading roles in British politics.

Another outstanding old boy, Winston Churchill, was less than happy at Harrow and did not do well academically. Other old boys, since the school was founded by John Lyon in the 16th century, include Robert Peel, Palmerston, Byron, Trollope and Lord Shaftesbury

Spectrum

♔ *His father's influence was apparent when Hussein was photographed* left *in the costume of a Bedouin ruler in 1945*

♔ *It was his late grandfather's influence that was paramount in the decision to send Hussein to Harrow School to complete his education. A fellow-pupil was his cousin, King Feisal II of Iraq* right, *with umbrella. Born in the same year as Hussein, Feisal became King at the age of four. He was assassinated during a rebellion in 1958*

He lived in 'Park', a house of 50 boys, and slept on a wood and canvas bed which served as a trouser press and had to be folded each morning. His closest 'friend' there was Miss Audrey Miskin, the house matron, who became his confidante. It was to her that Hussein poured out his fears about the growing threat to his homeland from the influx of refugees. And he shared with her his worries about his father's mental health, which was deteriorating despite constant medical treatment both in Jordan and Switzerland.

Life at Harrow

His housemaster described Hussein as 'a determined fellow, but limited in his academic ability.' He added, 'I would not say he was successful at Harrow, but we did what we could to equip him for the scramble we knew he would face in the Middle East.'

Although Hussein was not particularly good at games, he showed an enthusiasm and a determination that impressed his teachers, especially at rugby (a compulsory game) in which he 'would just put his head down and go in there and fight.'

Hussein had not been long at Harrow when his taste for fast cars and pretty girls began to show. Unlike other boys, he was allowed to

Hulton Picture Company

♔ *King Talal abdicated his throne in 1952, as his illness made him incapable of ruling. He travelled to Cairo* left *in the hope that Egyptian doctors might find a cure for his problems*

by the school, the young Harrovian, still only 16, was also seen occasionally at some of London's night-clubs. He was growing up quickly. Already the gossip columnists were taking note of his attractive girl companions. He usually arrived back at Harrow bearing a box of oriental sweetmeats, which he would share with his confidante, Miss Miskin.

Fast car, first love

One present from a friend of his father was a blue, supercharged Rover car that Hussein kept secretly at a garage near the school. Unknown to his housemaster or school-mates, the future King, like many an impetuous schoolboy, would drive this up to London or take it for a 'spin' around the countryside.

It was on such a spin to Cambridge that he

leave the school every weekend. A Jordanian Embassy Rolls would pick him up each Sunday and Hussein, still dressed in Harrow's Sunday uniform of black tail-coat, wing collar and striped trousers, would spend the day in the company of his own countrymen. The ambassador and his staff were aware that they were entertaining a future King and they looked after him well, showering him with presents.

On some weekends, given indulgent leave

♔ *Hussein was staying at the Hotel Beau-Rivage in Lausanne-Ouchy, Switzerland* right, *when he heard, by telegram, of his father's abdication. Soon after, he received a second telegram, in which Talal assured him of his continuing affection and asked him to make the Jordanian people happy. Prior to his call to the throne, Hussein had been enjoying himself in Switzerland driving a sporty red Bristol* below

Popperfoto

👑 *In September 1952, King Hussein visited Rome left. All traces of the carefree schoolboy had been left behind, and he had acquired a regal bearing. The instability of the Kingdom he had inherited was suggested by the revolver he wore on his hip*

👑 *Former King Talal's search for a cure took him from Egypt to Istanbul, where King Hussein visited him in 1953, staying at the Kuckusku Palace below*

in his terrible condition.

It was during this time that Hussein's housemaster received a mysterious visit from a high official at the Foreign Office. The official was Mr Geoffrey Furlonge, who was later to become British Ambassador in Jordan. He put one question to Mr Stevenson: 'Have you ever witnessed yourself or heard tell of any occurrence that leads you to believe that Hussein is mentally unstable in any way at all?'

The answer was simple. 'Certainly not,' said the teacher.

Hussein was on holiday from Harrow on Lake Geneva when he learned that he would become King. The date was 12 August 1952. He was 16 years old when a servant knocked on his hotel room door bearing a silver tray. The letter on it was addressed to 'His Majesty King Hussein' - even though Hussein was still not yet of age under Jordanian law.

met Dina Hamed, a distant cousin, who was studying at Girton College. They met at a party and Hussein realized that he was in love with this small and vivacious student. The love was not reciprocated, but Dina, seven years Hussein's senior, became a close friend for the rest of her cousin's stay at Harrow.

Father gets worse
In June 1952, Miss Miskin received a mysterious postcard at Harrow. It read: 'All my greetings and respects to you and Mr Stevenson [his housemaster] from Switzerland, with all hopes to return to Harrow as things are not doing so well now. Best wishes from Hussein.' His father's condition had worsened and Talal's knowledge, during his lucid moments, that he bore the responsibility for his kingdom added to his emotional burden. It was only a matter of time before Talal would be incapable of governing Jordan and Hussein would succeed to the throne.

Abdication
The following August, three Jordanian doctors declared Talal incapable of ruling. He was ordered to abdicate and did so readily, thanking his government for their past support. Talal retired to Egypt and later moved to an island in the Bosphorus, but there was no improvement

Topham

Lisa Halaby as a happy toddler in the USA

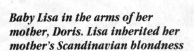

Baby Lisa in the arms of her mother, Doris. Lisa inherited her mother's Scandinavian blondness

Wearing her plaits in ribbons, Lisa, aged eight, poses with her father, Najeeb Halaby

Album

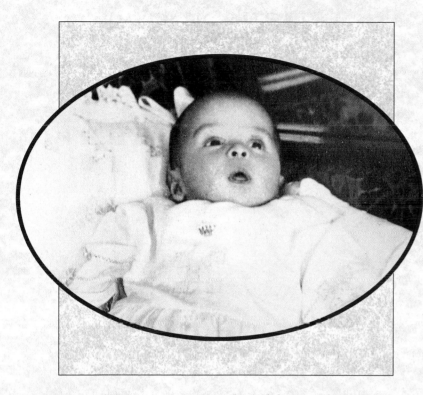

The young Prince was fond of cars from an early age

Prince Hussein bin Talal, pictured shortly after his birth in 1935

Hussein's enthusiasm for aircraft began as a boy. Here he stands by his first ever private aeroplane

Hussein, aged five, with his father and baby brother, Mohammed

ROYAL ORDERS & DECORATIONS

Jordanian Kings are inaugurated, not crowned, so King Hussein has no state regalia in the tradition of European monarchies. The inauguration itself is simply a ceremony which takes place in Parliament in which the new King swears an oath to uphold the constitution. Although there are no crown jewels, both the King and Queen wear an array of civil and military decorations and medals on formal or state occasions. The Queen, who has a collection of personal jewellery which is neither particularly extensive or very grand, tends to eschew the tiaras and necklaces favoured by other Royals

Tim Graham

👑 **Queen Noor wore this splendid set of turquoise and diamond earrings and necklace** *above* **to a state dinner during Their Majesties' 1987 visit to Paris. On state occasions both at home and abroad, the Queen rarely wears ostentatious jewellery**

Frank Spooner Pictures

👑 **King Hussein** *left* **addresses his guests during the state banquet given in honour of Queen Elizabeth II's visit to Jordan in 1984. The medals represent 12 Jordanian decorations, 12 Arab decorations and about 30 foreign decorations. The King also wears one of the highest British orders, the Star of the Order of the Bath, presented to him by Queen Elizabeth on this visit**

♛ This official portrait of King Hussein and Queen
Noor *above* was taken by the late Norman Parkinson,
one of the world's great Royal photographers. Both
the King and Queen wear the sash or Grand Collar of
Ali Hussein bin Ali and the Star of Ali Hussein bin Ali,
Jordan's highest decorations

IVY LEAGUE CHEERLEADER

THE DAUGHTER OF AN ARAB-AMERICAN AIRLINE EXECUTIVE, LISA HALABY DID WELL AT SCHOOL AND UNIVERSITY BEFORE BEING INTRODUCED TO THE KING AND TAKING A JOB WITH THE JORDANIAN AIRLINE

♔ *Lisa Najeeb Halaby was born on 23 August 1951 in the USA. Even as a baby right, she showed the charm and good looks that would later captivate a King*

I N 1953, AS HUSSEIN WAS ASCENDING ONE of the most dangerous thrones in the world, a green-eyed toddler with flowing fair hair was taking her first steps in a suburban street in Washington D.C. Her name was Lisa. The little girl was the daughter of an Arab-American father, Najeeb Halaby, and his Swedish-American wife, Doris Carlquist. Although it was her mother's striking Nordic looks that she inherited, Lisa was very close to her father in her early years.

Najeeb Halaby, a former president of Pan American Airlines, headed the Federal Aviation Administration during the Kennedy/Johnson years. He was one of the most powerful executives in the United States. It was a job which involved frequent travel. The family lived in Washington D.C., then moved to New York City and later to Los Angeles.

Lisa was, by her own admission, 'very shy and very pensive'. She was a loner and was rarely part of a large group. As a child, she read a great deal.

Syrian ancestry

Lisa was four years old and at kindergarten in New York when she learned that her father's ancestral roots were in distant Syria. She was oddly intrigued by the knowledge and spent much of her time questioning her father about Arab culture, customs and traditions. It was almost as though fortune was already beginning to link her with a handsome King in a far distant desert country.

She developed what she calls a 'very strong attachment' to her Arab roots and, as she grew older, she confided in her parents that she was sure that one day she would return to Arabia. 'It was a stubborn attachment that I can't explain because there's no logical reason, but I think it was something internal,' she later told one magazine writer.

Child of the sixties

Lisa was bright. She graduated with distinction from the Concord Academy in Massachusetts. At Princeton University, a traditionally all-male institution, Lisa was in the first class to include a small number of women. She surprised her friends at this prestigious, Ivy League university by wearing a black armband on her cheerleader's uniform in protest against the Vietnam war. She also took a fierce stand against America's involvement in the war in the college debating society.

Like so many children of the 1960s, Lisa Halaby was a Bob Dylan and Beatles fan. Completely emancipated, she was usually to be found in T-shirts and faded jeans, although when she attended official parties given by her parents, occasionally attended by the Ken-

'It was a stubborn attachment I can't explain ... but I think it was something internal'

LISA ON THE ATTRACTION OF ARABIA

♛ *Young Lisa grew up in what she later described as a 20th-century version of her Arab ancestors' nomadic way of life, as the exigencies of her father's job led the family above to move at intervals between Washington D.C., Los Angeles and New York*

♛ *Lisa was very close to her father in her early years. Whenever his job at the headquarters of Pan Am above allowed, he spent time with his daughter left, who continually questioned him about his Syrian origins and Arabic culture*

Gary Cralle/The Image Bank

15

PRINCETON

The small town of Princeton, New Jersey, houses one of the USA's oldest universities *below*. It was founded in 1746, and for the first 150 years was known as the College of New Jersey. It is one of the prestigious, long-established north-eastern universities (the others are Brown, Columbia, Cornell, Dartmouth, Harvard, Penn and Yale) which are known collectively as the Ivy League colleges.

Princeton's 2,200-acre campus was exclusively a male preserve until 1969, when Lisa Halaby was one of a handful of young women who became its first-ever female students. Its academic traditions are in the liberal arts and sciences, business studies and administration. One of the 20th century's most famous scientists, the German physicist Albert Einstein, was associated with the college during the last part of his life and died there in 1955

Patti McConville/The Image Bank

♛ *In 1968* above, *Lisa Halaby graduated from the Concord Academy, a private school in Massachusetts*

♛ *The future Queen entered Princeton in 1968 as part of the first-ever co-educational intake in the prestigious university's history* left. *At Princeton she took an active role in college life; she was a cheerleader for the football team and a frequent speaker at the debating society, where she spoke against the USA's military involvement in Vietnam, an issue which provoked mass demonstrations in the late 1960s and early 1970s* right. *She graduated in 1974, a poised and confident young woman with a glittering future ahead* top right

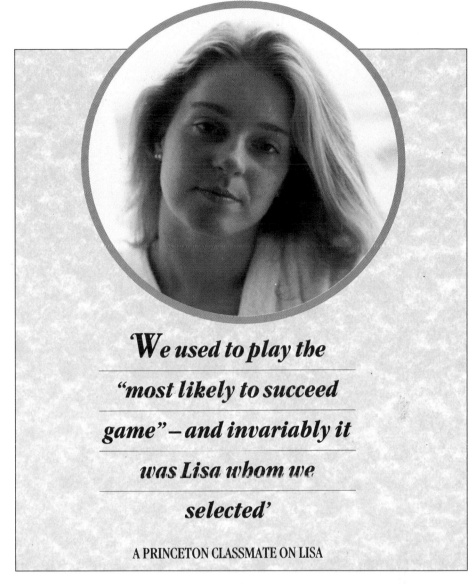

nedys or Rockefellers, she would be sure to wear her finest dresses.

'She was a popular girl,' reminisced one of her former classmates. 'She was both beautiful and vivacious and attracted a lot of attention from the men – although she was very selective in her choice of dates – staying popular with the girl students at the same time. She worked hard at her studies, but took part in most extra-college activities. We used to play the "most likely to succeed" game – and invariably it was Lisa whom we selected – if only for her energetic approach to everything from games to studies.'

Taking stock

She took a year's leave of absence from the university to attend a 'think tank' at Aspen, where she also took a course in photography and worked for a local architect. Many believed that she would end up as a photo-journalist but, even then, she was trying to determine her future career and decide what course she should study at Princeton.

She supplemented her income with a part-time job in Aspen as a waitress in a local diner. When she had made up her mind on her career direction she returned to Princeton. She graduated four years later with a degree in architecture and urban planning – 'a rich field in which one could explore anthropology, sociology, physiology, design and art, psychology and engineering,' she said.

Lisa was still fired with a desire to study the

We used to play the "most likely to succeed game" – and invariably it was Lisa whom we selected'

A PRINCETON CLASSMATE ON LISA

👑 *Lisa Halaby's talents with a camera led many of her university contemporaries to predict a career for her in photography. In 1975, she participated in the Australian National Photographic Index expedition to the rain forests of Queensland to photograph rare birds* above. *By 1978, Miss Halaby had settled in Amman* opposite page. *There, as an administrator at the airport, her path continually crossed that of King Hussein, who took a great interest in its development*

histories, customs and religions of the Middle East and South East Asia. She applied to the Graduate School of Journalism at Columbia University, where she planned to train as a writer specializing in socio-cultural relations. She was still in her early twenties. She was unattached, singularly beautiful and mature. The world was her oyster.

Travels abroad

Her choice of studies was to pay huge dividends in her role as Queen of a country far distant from the Princeton campus. Her skill as an architectural draughtswoman enabled her to travel the world, working and paying her way in travels to Iran, Thailand, Australia and Jordan.

She first visited Jordan in 1975 to see her father, who had formed his own international

civil aviation consultancy company. It was there that Lisa first came face-to-face with her future husband.

Najeeb Halaby and Hussein shared a common interest in developing aviation in the Middle East, and a long-standing friendship had grown between the two men. Mr Halaby introduced his daughter to the King at a reception and the two chatted briefly before the King moved on along the waiting line.

Working in Jordan

After having spent a year doing freelance research and design work in Jordan, Lisa was offered a post with Alia, the Jordanian national airline. The job was that of administrator with special responsibility for future development, particularly in the area of design. The small airport was to be enlarged and improved; a major challenge for Lisa Halaby's talents.

'She jumped at the opportunity,' said one airline official. 'Remember that she had spent much of her childhood and later working life on airplanes and almost living in airports. She knew every airport's failings and set out with a team to ensure that Amman airport was passenger-friendly as well as being, in her words, "the most efficient in the Middle East".'

National prestige

It was a period when many countries believed that their international status was judged by their airlines. Billions of petrodollars were invested in the new wide-bodied jets, with Boeing and other manufacturers offering substantial credit. Hussein subscribed to the importance of international prestige and Amman Airport and the Jordanian airline became his favourite projects. The airport was to play a significant part in Hussein's romantic life.

It was inevitable that his eyes should fall on the strikingly attractive blonde American girl once again.

ROYAL JORDANIAN AIRLINES

It was in the mid-1960s that the newly inaugurated *Alia Airlines* began flying regular scheduled services in the Middle East with a French Caravelle jet. Since then the King's 'pet project' has grown to such an extent that it flies to a far greater selection of destinations. Apart from the Middle East, the airline – now *Royal Jordanian Airlines* – flies to the United Kingdom, the USA, Canada and several destinations in the Far East. It operates a fleet of wide-bodied jets *right*, including 310 and 320 Airbuses

Royal Jordanian Airlines

Zebreh

AL NADWA PALACE

ROYAL RESIDENCE

The Royal couple's base in Amman is the Al Nadwa Palace, which lies within a stone-walled compound that runs from downtown out to the suburbs. Within the grounds is the Ma'wa, or Refuge, within which Queen Noor set up her offices. The Palace – a solid, unpretentious villa – has eight bedrooms for the King and Queen and their seven children

Rex Features

♛ Two lions *above* flank the red carpet at the main entrance to the Al Nadwa Palace. The square proportions of the white Palladian building are relieved by columns and archways leading onto open-air terraces at ground level. In one of the reception areas *left* the King and Queen are surrounded by fine Syrian craftsmanship. The furniture is damascened – inlaid with silver and mother-of-pearl

Rex Features

♕ The Palace is not air-conditioned and the bulletproof windows cannot be opened. In hot weather, meetings often take place on one of the terraces or patios. The Queen discusses a point *right* with her speechwriter on a terrace coolly furnished with modern black and white settees and glass-topped tables. White wrought-iron railings are a feature, and some windows have shutters in a similar style

Tom Stoddart/Frank Spooner Pictures

TROUBLED TIMES

**BEFORE ASSUMING THE CROWN, HUSSEIN WENT TO SANDHURST
AND HAD A BACHELOR'S LIVELY SOCIAL LIFE. HE WAS DESTINED
FOR MANY TURBULENT YEARS, WITH ATTEMPTS ON HIS LIFE
AND THREE MARRIAGES**

F ROM THE OUTSET, THE YOUNG KING KNEW that his rule of Jordan would be difficult. He had witnessed violence at first hand, and growing nationalism in the Middle East was to be a constant threat to the reigning Hashemite dynasty, whom many, particularly the highly vocal refugee community in Jordan, believed were no more than 'stooges' of the British.

There was a constant threat of a renewed war with Israel, with which Jordan shared a long and extremely vulnerable border. Abdullah had wanted his grandson to be a soldier, and now Hussein's government and his British advisers saw an urgent need for the country's leader to be trained as a warrior.

Within two months of leaving Harrow he was back in England, this time at the Royal Military Academy, Sandhurst, as an officer cadet. He was officially 'Cadet Hussein', but to Regimental Sergeant Major Lord, the man famed as having the loudest voice in the British army, he was 'Mr King of Jordan, sir!' Hussein proved to be an outstanding cadet during his six months at Sandhurst, delighting in night ex-

☞ *Officer Cadet King Hussein* above *spent six months at Sandhurst, passing out* below *in February 1953. The King particularly enjoyed the practical side of his military training such as drill, tactics, rifle shooting and mechanical engineering*

SANDHURST

It was King Hussein's uncle Sharif Nasser, an influential member of his family, who suggested a Sandhurst education. He was backed in this by the prime minister, Taufiq Abdul Huda.

The Royal Military College, near Camberley in Surrey, was established nearly 250 years ago under a Royal warrant. Sandhurst cadets, many of them graduates, undergo intensive courses of two or three terms. Apart from the inevitable 'square bashing', cadets are lectured on such varied subjects as the history of war, strategy, logistics and man-management. They also take part in manoeuvres with the army and other services. Their social behaviour is watched with equal concern by the staff.

Heirs to many thrones have graduated from Sandhurst. Among them have been the Sultans of Brunei and Oman and the late King of Iraq.

Although Regimental Sergeant Major Lord gave young Hussein a hard time on the parade ground, Hussein enjoyed his time at Sandhurst enough to fly to London to appear on a *This is Your Life* television programme in which his old RSM was the guest of honour

Popperfoto

ercises in the Surrey woods and readily absorbing complicated lectures on military history and modern tactics.

Living life to the full

Few of his friends and acquaintances in England realized the gravity of young Hussein's future, however. His passion for fast cars was growing; and he was rarely seen without a pretty girl close at hand during his weekends in London. The British Press tended to see him as no more than a playboy King, and some British diplomats despaired as Hussein was pictured

'He had all the qualities that Harrow and Sandhurst were built to foster – courage, resolution, enterprise . . .'

PETER SNOW ON THE YOUNG KING

racing through country lanes in a 120mph Aston Martin or buying a huge Lincoln convertible at the London Motor Show.

That was the public image of a 'playboy King'. Biographer Peter Snow saw another Hussein. 'The British educational establishment had produced a young leader it could be proud of,' he wrote. 'He had all the qualities that Harrow and Sandhurst were built to foster – courage, resolution, enterprise, a measure of self-assertiveness, a good practical judgement and the best public school manners. He persists, to this day, in calling men "Sir".'

👑 *While he was at Sandhurst, Hussein's name was linked with that of Princess Dina Abdul Hamed above left. She was older than the King and intellectually inclined, having been educated at Girton College, Cambridge and Cairo University. However, they enjoyed dancing together and shared a common Hashemite ancestry*

👑 *Hussein assumed the throne in May 1953 by taking the oath to the constitution in Parliament above. On his right are his younger brother, Crown Prince Mohammed and his uncle, Prince Naif. His mother, Queen Zein, waits discreetly in a side window below to see her son leaving Parliament after taking the oath*

Hussein's joy-riding and frequent night-club visits were carefully played down by the Press in his own country, and Jordanian newspapers remained discreet about the King's more serious attachments.

Romantic attachments

The King had often visited Dina Abdul Hamed in England and continued to court her even after he left Sandhurst to assume the throne of Jordan in May 1953. His name was linked with those of several women – including one famous British film star, Diana Dors. Hussein's attachment to Diana Dors – he had accompanied her to Edmundo Ros's London nightclub on several occasions – could well have caused an international scandal when letters of a passionate nature were hawked around Fleet Street. Whether they were from Hussein or not remains a matter of considerable doubt, but, suddenly, it was clear that the King of Jordan was no longer the innocent, curly-haired boy

23

Hulton Picture Company

♛ *Crowds line the streets of Amman* right *to cheer their new ruler. The inauguration ceremony in Jordan is traditionally followed by prayers in a mosque and an Arab-style banquet for distinguished guests*

♛ *On the day of his inauguration, King Hussein held an investiture for members of the Arab Legion, Jordan's defence force* below, *which at the time consisted of both British and Arab soldiers and was partly subsidized by the British government. Without British support in Jordan at this time, the balance of power in the Middle East would have been seriously upset*

Hulton Picture Company

whose large brown eyes had charmed his house matron. Hussein had reached manhood.

He was being talked about. Eligible girls — including one Italian beauty, Flavia Tesio, a doctor's daughter — were the subject of fervid gossip in Amman's close-knit society, but it was Dina who became Hussein's first Queen. He was 19, she was 26. She was a Hashemite Princess and shared Hussein's determination to maintain the Royal dynasty. Hussein had proposed to her by letter and she had accepted, even though she did not love the King. Hussein married Dina in 1955.

A failed marriage

It was not a successful marriage. Hussein wanted companionship, with a home and family that he could retire to from the affairs of state. Dina was not a home-maker; she was politically ambitious and caused resentment in royal and government circles by what was seen as interference. It took 18 months for the marriage to break down irrevocably and for Hussein to divorce his first love.

The divorce was not without rancour. Dina gave the Egyptian Press a hostile version of the reasons for the breakdown. Hussein's response was to insist on keeping their daughter, Alia, and for several years he refused Dina permission to even visit the child. Later on, in 1971, Dina was to marry a Palestinian commando called Salah — a fierce opponent of Hussein who had fought against her former husband's army.

A controversial sacking

Politically, Hussein was isolated in the turbulent Middle East. His cousin and only real ally, King Feisal of Iraq, had been assassinated in Baghdad; riots were raging in the streets of his own capital; and he had angered the British government by his peremptory sacking of his hero, Glubb Pasha.

A British magazine, *Picture Post*, had described Glubb as the 'uncrowned King of Jordan'. Hussein was furious, especially when Glubb tried to dismiss several of his leading officers for their nationalist beliefs. On the morning of 3 March 1956, Glubb Pasha, who had arrived in Jordan on a camel 32 years before, was told he was no longer required. By the following morning, he had left the country.

British hostility was not to last. When Hussein's kingdom was threatened, following a *coup* in Iraq, British paratroopers were flown into Amman at the request of the Jordanian Government. The presence of British troops on Arab soil infuriated Arab nationalists.

Attempts on his life

Between 1958 and 1960, Hussein survived four assassination attempts. The first of these took place in the air over Syria when Hussein, with Jock Dalgleish at the controls, found his Dove aircraft being 'buzzed' dangerously by Syrian MiG jet fighters. The royal plane escaped only by flying a few feet over the desert to escape radar tracking.

Later, while walking in the grounds of his Basman Palace, Hussein noticed a dead cat, then another two. The King had always insisted that his staff feed stray cats who wandered in. He learned that more than 12 dead cats had been discovered in the gardens. A palace cook confessed that he had been bribed to kill the King and was trying to establish the right dose of poison on stray cats.

A bomb exploded in the Jordanian Prime Minister's office at exactly the time Hussein was due. The premier died; Hussein was ten minutes late.

Soon afterwards, Hussein was warned of a plot to kill him in his own palace. The King has always suffered from sinus problems and discovered – just in time – that his nose drops had been replaced by concentrated nitric acid that would have killed him in an agonizing way.

Hussein rarely talked of this 'black side' of his rule. Freed from the bonds of marriage to Dina, he resumed the playboy role and was often seen – in Jordan and Europe – at the wheel of one of his stable of fast cars, always with an attractive woman at his side. Few could believe that this charming and lively man with dark, flirtatious eyes was in constant danger. Hussein, however, always carried a pistol. He had done so even at Harrow, ever since his grandfather's assassination.

It was at a fancy dress party that he was in-

Hulton Picture Company

🜲 *Both before and after his first marriage, the Press linked Hussein with a number of glamorous women. The film actress Diana Dors* above, *whom the King had taken to a nightclub in his Sandhurst days, was one*

Topham

🜲 *Hussein married Dina* left *in April 1955 when he was 19 years of age. Queen Zein had been keen on the match, possibly because she hoped her son would settle down and have a family but, despite the birth of a daughter, the marriage lasted only 18 months*

DAILY MAIL, Monday, August 11, 1958

A KING AT BAY

PRINCESS ALIA · PRINCESS BASMAH · QUEEN ZEIN · SHARIF NASSER

FAMILY MARKED DOWN FOR DEATH

Rex Features

troduced to Antoinette ('Toni') Gardiner, the daughter of one of Britain's military attachés in Amman. Although Toni was attractive, she lacked the uninhibited vivacity of most of Hussein's previous companions. Neither, unlike Dina, was she an intellectual in any sense. But she made up for that by a disarming frankness that appealed to the King. He was dressed as a pirate when they were introduced and allegedly her first words to him were 'You look pretty scruffy, Your Majesty.'

Deciding to marry

Spurning advice from both the British Embassy – concerned that it would look as though Britain had connived at the marriage – and his own ministers, Hussein resolved to marry the British girl and told a Press conference: 'My only nervousness about this marriage is that it is, to a great extent, a completion of a part of my life that has been missing.'

Hussein had no reason to be nervous. He and his bride, who was dressed in a wedding dress of pale cream wild silk studded with pearls and diamante, were cheered by the crowds as they drove through the streets of Amman. The date was 25 May 1961. Soldiers cried out 'Give our king a boy!' and hundreds of sheep were sacrificed and eaten as distant tribes celebrated.

Hussein made one major sacrifice, however. Knowing that a half-British son could hardly assume the throne of an Arab state, he named his brother Hassan as Crown Prince. Toni Gardiner, whom the ecstatic British popular Press had dubbed 'The Ipswich Typist', became Muna al Hussein ('the Choice of Hussein').

Four children

It was decided that Muna would be called 'Princess', rather than be given the title 'Queen'. She bore the King four children, Princes Abdullah and Feisal and twin girls, Zein and Aisha. It was Muna who finally reconciled Hussein with Dina, allowing the former Queen to visit Jordan to see her daughter.

The Arab King and his 'typically English' bride made a good match, with Toni offering the kind of homely companionship that Hussein had always wanted. She stayed carefully away from any involvement in Jordanian politics, but played a major role in improving the country's welfare services. Prudently, however, she always maintained a low profile.

The marriage lasted for 11 years, most of them contented. Nonetheless, the strain on Hussein, whose country was plunged into a bitter civil war in which much of Amman was either damaged or destroyed, was becoming intolerable. His life was under continual threat. In 1972, a renegade fighter pilot blasted his helicopter with rockets just before he boarded it. In 1977, a plot by rebel officers to shell the

Determined to assert his leadership over the Arab world, President Nasser of Egypt orchestrated several attempts on Hussein's life and that of his family above left *and* above. *That the King survived is partly due to the fierce loyalty of his Bedouin troops* below *and his own remarkable courage*

Loomis Dean/Camera Press

Camera Press

👑 *King Hussein's second wife, Princess Muna* left, *shared her husband's interest in the outdoor life and provided a necessary domestic tranquillity at a time when Hussein grappled valiantly with the continuing conflicts of the Arab world*

👑 *The King's third wife, Queen Alia, pictured* below *with their children, including an adopted daughter, gave the King not only love and companionship but fully supported him in his public duties and political life. He was utterly devastated by her tragic death*

The romance with Alia was truly a whirlwind one and Hussein lost no time in proposing to the striking beauty. 'He was like a little boy with a new toy,' said one friend of the family. 'He wanted to show Alia to everyone and toured the length and breadth of Jordan by car and helicopter to ensure that everyone should see his conquest.'

A love match

'He was bowled over by Alia's beauty,' said a Jordanian journalist. 'You could say that he was moon-eyed, quite obsessed with the woman.'

The two were clearly deeply in love when they married on the following Christmas Eve. Alia bore Hussein two more royal children, a Princess, Haya, and a Prince, Ali. They adopted a baby girl, Abir, who had been orphaned in an air crash. It was on a February evening in 1977 that Hussein, waiting at the airport to meet Alia, was told that her helicopter had crashed in a desert sandstorm and there were no survivors.

Palace from tanks was foiled after a tip-off.

It was this strain, and the arrival on the scene of a beautiful young public relations officer, Alia Toukan, at Amman Airport that finally ended the marriage. Hussein was in love with another woman, and made no secret of the fact.

'He was like a little boy with a new toy. He wanted to show Alia to everyone'

A FRIEND ON HUSSEIN'S NEW LOVE

There was no rancour involved in the separation from Muna. Hussein, who accepted responsibility for the divorce, made certain that Muna was well cared for.

She was given a palace in Amman – where she still lives with her parents – together with a house in Washington and a generous allowance as settlement. The only condition that Hussein imposed on her was that she should never talk about their relationship.

Many believe that Hussein's third marriage was the first true love match in his life – Lisa Halaby, of course, had yet to enter the picture.

Camera Press

♛ Although of Dior design and made in London, the stunning simplicity of Queen Noor's wedding gown *left* owes much to the easy, almost casual elegance of first-rate American dress design. Made of white silk crêpe, it is devoid of any glittering adornment or any show of ostentation – rather like the Queen of Jordan herself who admits that she selects her clothes not so much for herself as for 'the people I'm going to be with', on this occasion a group of family and friends

White crêpe wedding dress worn with a veil made of tulle, held in place with a headdress of leaves and lilies

Trailing bouquet of Arum lilies and ferns

♛ Noor wore this colourful garment of traditional Arabian design *right* at the Jerash Festival in 1984. The Queen has encouraged the revival of traditional crafts, among them textile weaving in patterns and colours similar to those on her rich and intricate bodice

This Christian Dior gown, beautiful in its simplicity, has wide pin-tucks at the hem and sleeves, decorated with fret work. This open work decorates the neckline too

The gown is softly gathered at the sleeves, and the bodice to the waistline, where the skirt falls into softly flowing folds

Lynne Robinson

TOP-CLASS NATURAL ELEGANCE

Queen Noor has a no-nonsense attitude to fashion and does not regard herself as an exceptionally fashionable person. 'If you really want to be fashionable, you have to have lots of time and energy, and I don't,' she explained. But, having said that, her natural elegance and almost instinctive sense of style place her in the top class of Royal dressers

♛ For formal or state occasions, Noor favours vibrant colours which complement her mane of golden hair and striking good looks. Like all her clothes, this evening gown is simple in design and elegant to wear

Royal blue outfit of lace. Bolero-style jacket of open lace, accessorised with rows of pearls at the neck, and drop pearl earrings

Rex Features

Sleeveless full-length dress with Spanish-style tiered skirt, in matching lined blue lace

Rex Features

Queen Noor can look particularly stunning in evening wear. This stylish black and red ensemble *left* was worn on a gala occasion during a visit to her home country. Note that the Queen wears no jewellery apart from earrings with the frilled and sequinned black top

Glittering evening gown with tightly fitting V-necked bodice, trimmed with a georgette frill at the neck-line

Black bodice studded with diamanté and clinched at the waist with a black satin belt with bow trim

Noor *above* looks wonderfully glamorous at the premiere of the film *Indiana Jones and the Last Crusade*. Her presence at the event was entirely appropriate since parts of the film were shot near Petra in Jordan

Floor-length red taffetta, bell shaped skirt

♛ This classic suit *left*, the design of which echoes the style of the painter Mondrian, was worn by Queen Noor when she bade farewell to Queen Elizabeth and the Duke of Edinburgh at the airport at the end of their highly successful state visit to Jordan

A very elegant 'Chanel style' suit with an unusual design, an inspiration from the artist, Mondrian

Jacket trimmed with black at the neck, button and cuff bands. The suit is completed with a slim-fitting black skirt

♛ Red is one of Queen Noor's favourite colours *right* but astrologers point out that this is hardly surprising since she was born on the cusp of Leo. Leos are known to love brilliant colours such as red and gold

Hoffman/Spooner

A NEW LOVE

THE TRAGIC DEATH OF HIS THIRD WIFE LEFT HUSSEIN A BROKEN MAN, BUT HE WAS REVITALIZED WHEN HE MET LISA AGAIN. A ROMANTIC COURTSHIP LED TO MARRIAGE, SEVERAL CHILDREN AND A HECTIC WORKLOAD FOR THE NEW QUEEN

HUSSEIN WAS PLUNGED INTO A BLACK depression after Alia's death. He is a soldier-king and an extrovert, who delights in the danger of high speed both in the air and on the roads, but he is also an emotional man, capable of being moved by grief. Alia's death affected him greatly.

In his anguish, Hussein turned to his ex-wife, Princess Muna, and her family and spent many tearful hours with them before plunging himself back into the affairs of state. Significantly, the Jordanians themselves admit that the great national love for Alia only took place after her death in such tragic circumstances.

Despite his obvious grief, the world's Press insisted on choosing his next bride for him. His name was linked romantically with a glamorous Disneyland guide, called Honey Rex, 23, and later with Margaret Trudeau, the estranged wife of Canadian Prime Minister Pierre Trudeau.

Airport romance

Hussein's main interests in Jordan at the time were the national airline and the country's international airport. Both were becoming increasingly busy as Beirut airport, once a major crossroads in the Middle East, was almost permanently closed by civil war.

At the beginning of 1976, Jordan's ministers and civic dignitaries lined up at Amman International Airport to greet the arrival of Jordan's first Jumbo jet. Hussein, radiant in his air force uniform, was presented to the line, but paused for more than the usual length of time when he was introduced to Lisa Halaby. It was clear to everyone present that the tall girl with long, honey-blonde hair had made an impact on the King.

He made frequent visits to the airport and it was not long before workers in the administrative office noticed that the King would make a detour on the way to the boardroom to pause in the office where Lisa Halaby was working. At first, their relationship was wholly professional, with

Zohrab

♔ *During the few short weeks of the engagement, Lisa lived in the Ma'wa, a small house in the grounds of the Palace which she later adopted as her office. When his duties permitted, Hussein would join her in walking in the grounds or spending time with his horses* above

♔ *Hussein also enjoys the power and speed of a metal steed* right. *While he was courting Lisa Halaby, they would ride out on one of his touring motorcycles, a more discreet form of travel than the limousines usually favoured by royalty and one which afforded a degree of privacy*

Carol Spencer/Frank Spooner

♛ *So discreet had been Hussein's and Lisa's courtship that the Press was taken unaware when news of the engagement broke. This photograph of Lisa as a student left was the only one to be found by the newspapers*

♛ *The King introduced his bride-to-be to the world at an official Press conference in May 1978, soon after their engagement was announced right*

♛ *The couple's wedding on 15 June 1978 was, as with all Muslim weddings, a relatively simple affair, taking just seven minutes. There was none of the pomp and pageantry traditionally associated with the marriages of reigning European monarchs. After making their vows before the witnesses, both signed a small book – the marriage contract – three times to seal their union below*

the King showing particular interest in Lisa's ideas for the airline's livery and her colour schemes for the passenger lounges and other buildings. He also invited her to come to the Al Hashemiah Palace to discuss structural problems throughout the building.

The courtship began with the King arriving at Lisa's flat in the centre of Amman at the wheel of one of his sports cars to take her to dinner at the Royal Palace. Subsequently, they spent much of the time travelling around the capital and through the countryside on a motorcycle.

These times together were probably the most private moments enjoyed by the couple during this period. Apart from the inevitable court gossips, however, few people realized that a true romance was in the air.

Love grows

Even today, the Queen remains discreet about the way the romance developed.

'Very spontaneously our friendship became something deeper,' she told one writer. 'It's all feelings. It's not something you can describe, really. Our relationship from the beginning has been totally spontaneous and instinctive for both of us. If you can believe that's possible for a King and a young girl ...but, in fact, it was exactly that. Had it been anything else, I don't think that we would be together.'

The courtship was discreet, partly because Hussein had never forgotten the international

D. Angeli/Camera Press

👑 *Both Hussein and his bride, the newly-named Queen Noor, wore Western dress for their wedding above and for their garden-party reception, a remarkably low-key affair to which only the couple's families and friends – including Princess Muna and her four children – were invited*

👑 *One of the few ostentatious features of the reception was the tall, many-tiered, pyramidal wedding-cake. In true military tradition, Hussein and his bride used a sabre to make the first cut*

fuss that attended his engagement to Toni Gardiner, another westerner. However, marriage to an Arab-American with the surname Halaby presented less of a problem.

The engagement

The ground was carefully laid for the announcement of the engagement. The first move was for Lisa to convert to the Islamic faith. This was not difficult for a girl who had studied Arabia and its customs so thoroughly. When King Hussein and Lisa Halaby became engaged, they decided to delay the public announcement for several weeks to allow Lisa to travel to the USA or Europe to prepare for the wedding with her family.

However, the following morning, the King, unable to contain his emotions, confided in a cousin at the Royal Court. The secret was out and announced officially soon after.

Hussein, who had been almost a broken man less than 18 months before, was ecstatic. 'My life has been full of tragedy,' he said. 'She has brought me a strength and happiness I didn't believe possible to find again.'

Almost overnight, Lisa was moved from her small apartment in Amman to the Ma'wa, or Refuge, an old house in the grounds of the Royal Court office compound. There she lived until the day of her wedding.

Hussein and Lisa married in June, 1978. A Moslem wedding service is a simple, almost austere, affair governed by Islamic law. The King, sporting a grey 'designer' beard and wearing a dark blue Savile Row lounge suit, and his bride, who wore a simple white dress, sat in front of a low coffee table in the Royal Palace. They were

Frilet/Rex Features

asked by Sheikh Ibrahim Catan, Chief Justice of the Moslem Sharia Court, the supreme religious authority in Jordan, whether they took each other as man and wife.

An Arabic service

The service was conducted in Arabic and, although Lisa had studied this difficult language more than most westerners, she found it difficult to give the short acceptance. Perhaps the once-so-liberated girl was nervous when she answered, 'I have betrothed myself to thee in marriage for the dowry agreed upon.'

Both answered 'Na'am' ('yes' in Arabic) to a final question, Hussein responding in his deep, guttural voice and Lisa still betraying a trace of her American accent. The Sheikh then took a small book to both. Hussein signed three different pages on the left hand side and Lisa signed three pages on the right. The only witnesses were men – another Moslem tradition – who shouted 'Mabrak!' ('congratulations').

Then it was the women's turn to greet the

'She has brought me a strength and happiness I didn't believe possible to find again'

HUSSEIN ON LISA

newly married couple. Hussein led Lisa, who was wearing flowers in her hair, into an ante-room where Queen Zein and Mrs Halaby were waiting with the Royal Princesses. Lisa wore little make-up, but her ear-rings were sparkling with diamonds, as were the bracelets she wore on her wrists.

A new name

Rose petal drinks were passed round, followed by tea in which the party toasted Hussein and his bride. It was only then that Hussein revealed the Arabic title that Lisa Halaby would assume. From that day on, she would be 'Noor Al Hussein' – 'the Light of Hussein'.

The couple left for a brief honeymoon on the Red Sea at Aqaba and a short visit to the Scottish Highlands. Honeymoon plans to visit the Majorca home of King Juan Carlos and Queen Sofia of Spain were curtailed by events in the Middle East.

On her return Queen Noor determined that there would be no comparison in the world's thirsty tabloids between her and her glamorous compatriot, the late Princess Grace. Such a com-

👑 *King Hussein's wedding present to his new bride was a suitably beribboned American classic car, a pre-war Panhard* right

👑 *After their wedding, the Royal couple travelled to the Jordanian resort of Aqaba, on the Red Sea, then flew to Gleneagles in Scotland* below. *The projected third leg of their honeymoon, in Majorca, had to be abandoned owing to political unrest in Jordan at the time*

Frilet/Rex Features

Photographers International

♛ *Queen Noor has been careful to present heself to her new country as something much more than a glamorous consort to the King. Formal portraits, such as those taken by Norman Parkinson in the first year of her marriage* right *are rare: she is much more often to be seen in situations related to the work on behalf of the people of Jordan that she has undertaken through the Noor al Hussein Foundation*

♛ *One of the Queen's projects is to promote the revival of the production of textiles in Jordan's villages. This not only helps to preserve the traditional skill of weaving, but also provides much-needed income for women in rural areas* below

Norman Parkinson

George Crystal

parison would have been dangerous in staid, conservative Jordan where many women still walked at the appropriate number of paces behind their menfolk.

The right image

She spurned interviews and did nothing to court publicity unless it was in Jordan's interest. The image she chose to present to her husband's people was that of a hardworking, dedicated and businesslike woman, subordinate to Hussein in all their public appearances, and serious and dignified at all times.

Although the Royal couple had never fully discussed Noor's role after their marriage, the Queen sought an opportunity to use the skills she had learned at university. She was anxious to avoid involvement in internal politics, like her predecessor, Muna, and to add a much-needed American dimension of practicality to Hussein's rule over his troubled country.

Her problem was how to steer clear of politics and avoid the inevitable resentment of Hussein's ministers at what they would certainly see as interference, no matter how well-intentioned. Noor set out to concentrate on a much neglected and non-controversial aspect of Jordanian life — the country's culture. Years of war and tension had almost smothered it. At a time when worldwide tourism was burgeoning, Jordan had two remarkable and unspoilt jewels to show the world — Petra, the city carved from rock, in the south, and the superb Graeco-Roman ruins to the north of Amman.

The Queen's projects

Queen Noor organized an annual Culture and Arts Festival in the ancient Roman city of Jerash. A feature of this were performances of Western classical music, in splendid settings. Alongside the performing arts were displays of locally produced fabrics — Noor was largely responsible for planning a new textile industry in her country — and other Jordanian products.

It was the intense energy and enthusiasm which Noor gave to these projects that won her the affection of even the most sceptical of Jordanians. Before long, the new Queen had taken on a huge workload which was organized from offices in a small building near the Royal Court. These development projects were eventually placed under the umbrella of the Noor Al Hussein Foundation. Noor has been closely involved in the planning of the Jubilee School, a boarding school for 200 gifted scholarship children from all areas of the Kingdom of Jordan.

Her foundation is also involved in the creation of new health clinics, much-needed orphanages and various conservation schemes. She has involved herself in setting up village handicraft projects, family planning clinics and, because half the population of Jordan is under the age of 15, a pediatric hospital in Amman. Such is that workload that Noor needs two secretaries, an American and a Jordanian, who usually start work with the Queen before 7am each morning.

George Crystal

♛ *Queen Noor is also involved in the educational field, taking particular interest in the schooling of girls* above, *which was rarely undertaken in Muslim societies until relatively recently*

A LAND OF HISTORY

Queen Noor has been a key figure in building up Jordan's not inconsiderable tourist industry over recent years. Much of the country is inhospitable mountain and desert terrain, but Jordan certainly has its tourist jewels. The country is exploiting them to the full with new roads, luxury hotels and even a school where young Jordanians are taught the finer points of service.

The country does have a remarkable history. Long before Christ it was the crossroads and meeting place for numerous civilizations. The Hittite, Roman, Greek and Byzantine empires have all left their mark. Apart from Petra, one of the most visited places is the Graeco-Roman city of Jerash ('the Pompeii of the Middle East'). It holds an annual international festival of music and the arts inspired by Queen Noor herself *right*. Many of the world's leading solo musicians and orchestras have played at this festival.

Another famous attraction is the Wadi Rum, with its superb desert moonscapes — featured so effectively in the film *Lawrence of Arabia*

Zohrab

It is not unusual for a helicopter to land in the grounds of a distant village school and for Noor herself to meet the children and staff. She listens to their problems and needs and discusses possible solutions.

Winning over the people

In the 12 years since Noor became Queen, she has stamped her personality on the country in a way which has frankly amazed many Jordanians. A member of the Jordanian Embassy staff

> ## 'Many people believed that an American Queen could not possibly succeed . . . she has achieved a great deal'
>
> JORDANIAN DIPLOMAT

in London put it this way: 'Many people believed that an American Queen could not possibly succeed in our country. In fact, Her Majesty's work in the social and educational fields was desperately needed and will bring long-lasting benefits to Jordan. She has achieved a great deal, always with a true queen-like dignity, and has inspired many people to work

together in the common cause.'

In Jordan itself, Noor maintains a high profile and rarely a day passes when she is not seen at any one of a hundred different functions in the country. The paradox is that she is one of the least known Royal personages on the wider international scene.

She travels abroad to lecture on Middle East politics and to promote greater interest in, and understanding of Jordan. Her speeches are

In the last decade, Queen Noor has divided her time between her large and growing family and her public duties. Her fourth child, Princess Raiyah above left, was born in 1986. In 1984, the Queen left Jordan to undertake an important lecture tour of the USA. At the World Affairs Council in California above she spoke on the theme 'Principles of Democracy: Jordan's Road to Peace'

ANCIENT PETRA

It was not until the middle of the last century that a Swiss explorer rode through a gorge in the southern Jordanian mountains and found an extraordinary city *right*. Its villas, temples, markets and tombs were carved entirely from the rock face. He had discovered Petra (meaning 'rock'), a city built at least 100 years before Christ by the energetic Nabataeans. They were a nomadic tribe who created a huge trading empire in Arabia, and Petra became the centre of the caravan trade in incense, myrrh, pearls, spices, cotton and Chinese silk.

The city was celebrated with these lines by Dean Burgeon:

'Match me such marvel save in Eastern clime,
A rose red city "half as old as time".'

Only recently has the city become a key tourist attraction. A main road has been opened up and thousands of visitors are able to marvel at the beauty of Petra

Tom Deas

Zohrab

👑 *Jordan places a high premium on youth. As well as educational projects and literacy programmes, King Hussein and Queen Noor also support more general ventures, such as the National Youth Festival in Amman* above

👑 *In 1990, Queen Noor was helped by her daughter, Raiyah, when she planted trees to celebrate Earth Day* below

on a family and a country,' she says. 'So it's not the same thing as a public figure or someone who has not got this extraordinary combination of responsibilities.'

'When I speak . . . it reflects on a country'

QUEEN NOOR

George Crystal

known to be quite frank and direct which has, at least on one occasion, caused some discomfiture at the State Department in Washington D.C. She is much in demand as a public speaker, particularly in the United States. In recent years, however, her work on domestic issues in Jordan has prevented her from accepting many invitations. Nevertheless, she lectured in 1987 at Oxford University and at various other major international venues since then.

Controversy and diplomacy

Although her international role has brought criticism from extremists in her adopted country, she is supported by many who value her potential as a unique bridge between the Arab world and the West. Noor herself is very much aware of her role as an ambassador for Jordan and she chooses her words with care.

Noor will often re write a speech as many as 20 times before she is satisfied. 'If you have noticed me trying to be careful about how I stress things, it's because when I speak or am quoted, it doesn't just reflect on me, it reflects

FAMILY MOMENTS

State business has to come first but whenever possible the family tries to be together. Many of their treasured moments and favourite photographs are of family occasions. These are often at home in Amman or on holiday in Aqaba or abroad, when they frequently play sports together. The children are reaching an age when they can join State occasions with their parents

♛ The King is seen *above* at Amman Airport on the occasion of Queen Noor's 33rd birthday in August 1984. Keen to be with their father and to explore his helicopter are Prince Hamzah and, on the tarmac, the 18-month-old Princess Iman. King Hussein and Queen Noor hold three-year-old Prince Hashim and baby Princess Iman *left*, outside their home at Aqaba in 1984

♛ Aqaba is a great favourite with the family as there is plenty of opportunity for sailing and powerboating. Queen Noor, with her sons, *above* takes the wheel of a speedboat, though Prince Hamzah is the nominal driver

Kennerly/Frank Spooner Pictures

Tender To **NOOR**

♛ Queen Noor and her father, Najeeb Halaby, enjoy a chat *left* in the tender on board the Royal motor yacht named after the Queen. Her Majesty also enjoys skiing, and has introduced her children to the pleasures of the slopes at a young age. In February 1988, she carries her youngest child, Princess Raiyah, who is not yet two but is already learning to master skis *below*

Fevrier/Rex Features

George Crystal

♛ King Hussein and Queen Noor on a visit to the excavation of the Islamic City of Aqaba. They are accompanied by Princes Hamzah and Hashim and by Princess Iman, who is avidly looking at an album of photos recording the progress of the archeological dig

A HOMELY PALACE

**THE ROYAL PALACE IS A FAMILY HOME FULL OF CHILDREN, WHERE
THE ROYAL COUPLE CAN RELAX. IN OFF-DUTY MOMENTS THEY PLAY
SPORTS OR VISIT THEIR HOLIDAY HOMES AT AQABA AND ASCOT**

♛ Jordan's glamorous Queen leads a full and active life both at home and abroad. She is patron of several organizations, among them the International Union for the Conservation of Nature and Natural Resources, which she addressed left on the occasion of its 40th anniversary in October 1988 in Paris. At home she combines her duties as a Queen with those of a mother and a loving wife to King Hussein opposite top left.

As part of her duties as Queen, Noor visits the underdeveloped rural areas of Jordan. When she visits Bedouin villages, she receives petitions on behalf of her husband opposite above right. Jordan is a constitutional monarchy in which the sovereign has a good deal of executive power, and many of his subjects prefer to petition the King directly if they have any problem.

However, the Queen's main interest is her growing family opposite main picture. Queen Noor has Princess Iman on her lap, while Prince Hamzah sits beside his father. In front sit left to right Princess Haya and Prince Ali, the children of Queen Alia, Prince Hashim, and Miss Abir Muhsaisen, the young orphan adopted by Hussein and Alia

NOW IN HER LATE THIRTIES, THE FORMER Lisa Halaby remains slender and eminently attractive, and radiates good health. Her workload is prodigious, and yet she has borne Hussein four more children, Prince Hamzah, Prince Hashim, Princess Iman and Princess Raiyah. She has also raised Queen Alia's three children. It is perhaps the presence of so many children that makes the Royal Palace such a lively and happy place – for that is the impression most visitors take away with them.

The Al Nadwa Palace itself is a modest, almost austere, building of sandstone, standing in superb gardens with a private zoo in one cor-ner. Surprisingly, despite the intense heat of the Jordanian summer and the fact that the Queen is American, the palace is not air-conditioned. The main drawing room, which also serves as a reception room for distinguished visitors, is cosy, friendly and very much a family room. Its walls are lined with inscribed photographs of Royal families and heads of state – including a particularly large one of Margaret Thatcher.

Stylish clothes

In public, Noor wears stylish, though conservative clothes, often opting for straight skirts and peplum jackets, for instance. She favours a traditional Arab caftan on ceremonial occasions, but enjoys visiting villages wearing simple white shirts, khaki skirts and boots.

At home with her children she favours blue jeans and cotton shirts but will never be seen wearing them in public, or be photographed in them. 'Because we are a conservative country, I don't think the image of their Queen in jeans is really something that the people here would be comfortable with,' she told one visitor. 'On the other hand, they wouldn't feel comfortable if my image were only glossy or glamorous either. I think the image that most Jordanians would like to have of their queen is of someone who is serious and dedicated and businesslike.'

A family home

Visitors are made welcome, usually with iced soft-drinks or tea, served in the drawing room in winter or on the terrace in the summer; but the upstairs at Al Nadwa is strictly out of bounds. The palace had to be enlarged to cope with the Royal children and there are eight bedrooms, seven for the children and a main bedroom for the King and Queen.

Noor insisted from the outset that the children should be close to their parents and not compartmentalized in other parts of the palace.

Zohrab

Terry O'Neill

Tim Graham

'I know this is not the case for some other families in our position, but I'm determined that we should have as much of a family life as possible,' she told friends.

Time for the children

Noor devotes as much of her time as possible to the children. She has devised weekly schedules for each of them, ensuring that they attend their music lessons or special studies and that she and the King are always available for their confidences at given times. An English and a Jordanian nanny look after the children while their mother and father are working. At Noor's insistence, the children go to local schools, despite the security headaches this involves.

English and Arabic are spoken equally. Noor, who spoke only halting phrases in Arabic when she was married, is now wholly fluent in her husband's language. She prides herself that she is equally fluent in written Arabic, so much so that she can decipher even the most delicate *nuances* in the kind of petitions she is handed during her visits to her people.

Noor can be quite strict when it comes to the children's TV watching habits. 'I discourage too much television and junk food and the children staying up all night,' she says. 'I am the dis-

The love of King Hussein and his Arab-American Queen continues to grow stronger and more secure above left. Ever since their honeymoon, the north of Scotland has held a special place in their affections, and both of them like to return there when time permits above right

'*I'm determined that we should have as much of a family life as possible*'

NOOR

ciplinarian of the family, yes – but because of the extended nature of our family, it's impossible to have any consistent control.' As for their schooling she adds: 'I try to insist they are treated exactly the same as anyone else. It doesn't always work out that way, but I try....'

She can be frugal, too. In the winter she will tour the palace, turning off unwanted lights – and the Royal children are expected to wear each others' 'hand-me-downs'.

Sporting interests

Noor encourages physical activity and it is not unusual for almost the entire family to join her in games of tennis, horse-back riding or her regular thrice-weekly aerobic workout to western rock music. Hussein, however, prefers to watch. He has succeeded in interesting his wife in classical Arabic music but is himself perhaps even keener on western classical music. She, in turn, has persuaded him to enjoy Country and Western music.

A home by the sea

In the summer, the royal couple spend as much time as possible at their seaside home at Aqaba. They have a pleasant brick-built cottage there with several small chalets in the Royal com-

♛ *The whole Royal Family are keen on sport. Though Hussein prefers these days to take on the role of a spectator, he reflects his English education in playing the occasional game of cricket left. Queen Noor's wide-ranging sporting interests include tennis, and she is quite likely to include much of the family in a game of doubles below*

'*I try to insist*

they are treated

exactly the same

as anyone else'

NOOR ON HER CHILDREN

CLASSIC POWER

King Hussein has had a passion for powerful, sporty motor cars ever since he was given a sky-blue Rover while still a schoolboy at Harrow. When he was looking for a garage for this, Hussein met Maurice Raynor, an English car enthusiast and skilled mechanic. Raynor became a personal friend and later moved to Jordan to run the Royal garages.

Hussein now owns and drives *below* one of the world's finest collections of Classic cars. Speed remains his primary interest pound for guests. Noor enjoys 'just being so close to the sea.'

Noor's passion for sport was one thing that attracted Hussein to her. In addition to aerobics and jogging, she loves water-skiing and sailing. She also plays a powerful game of tennis and is keen on flying.

Aqaba is one of the few places in the country where Noor feels she can be alone in safety. She rebelled when she found her Laser dinghy being followed by security gunboats. She can

'A little cottage, lost in the mountains'

NOOR'S DAYDREAM

drive freely into the desert, too, in her Mercedes four-wheel drive jeep, usually with music at full volume on her stereo player.

Close to the Windsors

For their visits to Britain, usually in springtime, they have a typical English country house. It was presented to them by friends and is near Ascot. Their land borders Windsor Great Park and Queen Elizabeth and Prince Philip are close neighbours when at Windsor Castle.

♛ *Aqaba, lying on an arm of the Red Sea between Sinai and Arabia, is a favourite resort of the Royal Family* below. *Their palace there resembles a grand beachfront villa* left. *On occasions, the car-loving King can be persuaded to exchange four wheels for two. On a visit to England in 1987, Hussein and Noor took their youngest child, Princess Raiyah, for a spin in the countryside* right above. *In June 1990, Their Majesties took time out to watch a hill climbing race* right below

The Ascot home is no more than a base, however, for their true love is touring in Scotland. They are particularly fond of the Isle of Skye, where they spent part of their belated honeymoon. Even on these private trips they are generally followed by an unmarked car, filled with watchful British and Jordanian secret servicemen. An exhausted Noor once confided that she yearned for 'a little cottage, lost in the mountains.'

Pluses and minuses

Noor once told an interviewer: 'You ask if I miss anything by being Queen. Just the privacy and the simplicity — and doing things for myself, even going out for groceries. Sometimes I think that what others regard as the most mundane parts of their lives are what I yearn for. But on the other hand, I wouldn't trade my life's offerings for anything. I see what life has offered, not what it has taken away.

'Being Queen has given me the freedom to make use of one's life in a humanitarian way — something I'd always dreamed of. It was my husband's choice and my choice. Together, we can achieve a lot, God willing.'

Noor's own style

Some royal observers have compared Noor with the British Queen, but the Queen of Jordan would firmly deny modelling herself on Queen Elizabeth. Noor is, nevertheless, always immaculately turned out and expertly coiffeured on any public occasion. At the Jordanian officer corps' passing out parade, the nearest equivalent to the British trooping of the colour, she wears a military uniform. Noor, too, can look spectacularly regal at civic functions,

Zohrab

♔ *On occasion – particularly for the Jordanian officer corps' passing out parade – Queen Noor abandons her usual immaculately feminine clothing for a military uniform* left

♔ *The high-society visit of Queen Elizabeth II of England and the Duke of Edinburgh to Jordan in 1984 was a personal triumph for Noor, who was largely responsible for planning it. One of the highlights of the visit was a trip to Petra in the Dead Sea basin, where the Royal party drank mint tea in a Bedouin tent beneath the watchful eye of a heavily-armed guard* below

John Shelley

dressed in a ballgown sparkling with jewels; but there the comparison ends.

It is quite likely that no more than a few hours before making that regal appearance, Noor will have been squatting at eye-level with children in one of the country's tented villages. Or she may have been sitting on traditional cushions in a tent, receiving petitions from Bedouin women about such mundane subjects as water supplies or their need for health clinics.

Security headaches

One constant factor attends the King and Queen of Jordan at all times. There is always an armed security guard close at hand wherever they happen to be.

Security was never more stringent in Jordan than during the state visit by Queen Elizabeth and the Duke of Edinburgh. Two days before the Royal visitors were due to arrive, a

> **'Being Queen has given me the freedom to make use of one's life in a humanitarian way – something I'd always dreamed of'**
>
> NOOR

small bomb exploded in an Amman hotel car park, causing little damage but stirring a flurry of political concern.

Mrs Thatcher was concerned and called an emergency cabinet meeting at Chequers. Calls went out to King Hussein and the tour seemed in danger of cancellation until Queen Elizabeth insisted that it should go ahead.

A massive guard surrounded the Royal couples at all times. Land-rovers bristling with machine guns escorted the bullet-proof Mercedes at high speed along desert roads. The visit was judged a success – although, sadly, the British royals had few opportunities of meeting ordinary Jordanians.

Few realized that much of the planning of the visit had been done by Queen Noor. The woman who, but a few years ago, had been a student in an American university had grown fully into her new role as Queen. Hussein was said to be 'very proud' of her.